How to Become a Model

The Ultimate Guide to a Successful Modeling Career as a Professional Model

by Liza Jo Laney

Table of Contents

Introduction

The fashion industry is incredibly picky about the faces of their brands and products. However, if you have "the look", and the desire to be a model, then this may yet be a great opportunity for you. Today, the robust growth of the fashion and beauty industry has opened up countless opportunities for many people, even for those who don't consider themselves particularly beautiful in the conventional sense. The fashion industry has even started expanding its horizons to consider factual representations of women which were traditionally avoided, as exemplified by the rise in number of "plus–size" models.

In this book, we will give you all the necessary information on how to become a model; including how to get started, how to choose the right agency, how to hone your talent, and how to back all that beauty with skill and charisma - the two most important things for attracting public attention. We will also show you how to come up with an "exit strategy", since you won't be a model for the rest of your life. Furthermore, we'll teach you how to establish a career as a professional model – anyone can be a one-hit wonder, but establishing a long-term portfolio in this industry requires smarts more than sass, and networking more than diva-hood.

As a first step, if you wish to progress along this path, the motto you need to live by from on is - While being beautiful, slim, tall and having curves in all the right places is great, if it isn't backed by hard work, determination and proper training, I'm not going to become the next Naomi.

So, if you want to become a successful model then this book will guide you through your first steps. Without further ado, let's get started!

Chapter 1: Preparing to Become a Model

If a model has to be slim, that does not mean that he or she has to be anorexic. You will need the energy to go for long duration photo shoots, and often stand in uncomfortable positions in locations with taxing temperatures. Besides, the fashion industries in several countries such as France and Italy have drafted and cemented agreements to stop signing on "minus-size" models, since they have deemed it important to impart a healthy representative outlook of today's women rather than stick to the biases perpetuated through fashion till date. Also, you will never get a gig if you look sickly. Optimum body health is compulsory. In this chapter, we will focus on a few tips to ensure that you get - and maintain - a model's physique and, most importantly, health.

Skin care is paramount. Flawless, healthy, well moisturized skin is essential for this job. It is important to exfoliate few times a week, and wash your face every morning and at night. If you wear makeup, then wash it off before going to sleep. However, an important point here is that a healthy diet will translate to healthy skin. So don't skimp on fruits, green vegetables and sufficient amounts of water every day. This attribute applies to all models, be they fashion or glamour, plus size or traditional. Your skin needs to be healthy, blemish-free and as hairless as possible. Additionally, you need to take special care of the health of your hair as well. While some gigs may specifically call for greasy hair, in most cases unkempt hair would get you rejected out of hand.

Fitness is crucial – Just because you are thin does not mean you are fit. You need to work with a trainer who can help you stick to a sound workout schedule. Find a trainer who works with models and tell him/her you want to be a professional model. Avoid any heavy weight-oriented regimes, and concentrate on cardio-vascular strength, flexibility, and muscle-toning for women (the first two attributes and lean muscle building for men).

Eat right. The health of your digestive tract, and the nutrient balance of your foods, directly impacts your outer beauty – therefore avoid unnecessary sugars and starchy foods. Instead, concentrate on healthy whole grains, balanced quantities of proteins, vegetables and dairy products, as well as required amounts of nutritional supplements to keep your energy at peak levels.

Always have enough sleep. If you don't, it will show through your eyes and skin. Did you know that lack of sleep promotes fast aging and reduces skin elasticity? In addition, when you are asleep, the body is able to rid itself of the free radicals that contribute to skin damage.

There are no preferences for skin color and tone in modeling, but it must be very smooth and without a blemish anywhere. It doesn't matter whether you are a supermodel or not, no one can overemphasize the importance of flawless skin and hair. When taking close-up photographs to take to modeling agencies, don't wear too much makeup. The agent will be looking at the quality of your skin. Up to a point, the rule should be the less the makeup you wear, the better. In fact, the better you look as a natural beauty, the more your chances of making it big faster over other more established models who need to rely on make-up more than you do.

Is smooth skin important for male models? What about their body hair? There are no two ways about this, if you want to become a model, you must have no body hair. For example, if you are a body part model where a company wants to use your feet for their shoes, you must have hairless feet. In addition, basic skin care that most men adopt (a quick early morning wash with 3-in-one products) will simply not do. You will have to make time for extra self-primping. Most male models usually put aside time for facials and/or body packs, with meticulously chosen face scrubs and washes which they use in rigorous daily grooming schedules.

Male models should work out quite often. A set of abs is almost imperative, but certainly at least we can say it's a big bonus, for male models. Their hair can be any length, up to a point. Men should take good care of their hair because, in this industry, hair and skin are everything. Take care of your nails too: they should be short, neat and well manicured. Sometimes it is the little things that make all the difference.

Chapter 2: Choosing Your Style of Modeling

When pursuing a modeling career, there are many kinds of modeling that you can do, and you need to figure out which one is right for you.

FASHION MODELING

Fashion modeling is probably the best known type of modeling work. As a fashion model, you will be the face and body behind products like lingerie, clothes, eye-wear, perfumes and shoes among others. To become a fashion model, you will need to meet certain attributes like aesthetic facial attributes, pleasing body structure, rigorous levels of fitness, unique "look" (look in your eyes or face while you walk the ramp, rather than just your basic looks), etc.

Under the category of fashion models, there are several different types of modeling. They include runway, catalog, editorial, and fit modeling. Within a successful fashion modeling portfolio, you should be able to try these all during your career.

Attributes of a female fashion model

Traditional female models are usually "scouted" between the ages of 17 and 21, with body shapes that range within variations of 34-24-34. While they are usually between 5'9" and 6'0" tall, with weight ranging between 105-130 pounds, the weight range may vary as long as the model looks fit and well-proportioned dependent on her height.

Attributes of a male fashion model

Male models usually start their careers between 18 and 25 years old, with heights between 5'10"1/2 and 6'2". Although their waist size should be between 29" to 32", with weights between 140 to 165 pounds, their weight range may vary depending on their muscular development and aesthetic physical proportions. However, the fashion industry may also have certain preferences with regards to sleeve sizes and neck sizes, so it's not recommended to bulk up a lot during muscular development, since you may not fit into clothes prepared by most designers after such an eventuality.

COMMERCIAL PRINT MODELING

This second modeling category is used for the promotion of companies, products and services. It is a bit more flexible because there is no set height limit for models, but the industry can still be very selective in other ways. Models must be proportionate and attractive, and most importantly, should be able to play different characters, similar to acting. Fitness of body and skin are still paramount though, even if commercial print would allow use of photo-shop software – since the more you reduce the extra work needed to be done by others, the higher the chances of you developing regular gigs with clientele.

Swimwear, fitness, lingerie, corporate and glamour modeling are just a few of the subcategories that fall under this kind of modeling.

BODY PART MODELING

This type of modeling focuses on a part of the body. It could be hand modeling, where the fingers should be long and slender, hairless and with no blemishes on the skin. Or it could be the neck, long and graceful. There are really as many categories as you can think of, with everything from feet to ears to hair.

However, with few exceptions, body part modeling as a field often serves as odd jobs for commercial or fashion models, rather than exclusive body part models.

COMMERCIAL MODELING

This is not fashion or glamour modeling, but it is very wide in scope. Thus, the physical attributes also vary a lot. The model could be a mom, granddad, scientist, business person and so forth. While the pay is not as good as you would get in fashion modeling, it is still worthwhile, and the industry is not as strict on looks.

Some of the categories that fall into this commercial category include commercial product modeling, commercial lifestyle modeling, commercial corporate modeling, and trade show modeling, among others.

GLAMOUR MODELING

This is a kind of modeling that is done for photos with a sensual theme. However, note that while this kind of modeling may be sensual in nature, it is not pornographic. Bikini and lingerie modeling mostly fall into this category – which require aesthetically pleasing or captivating body proportions, rather than focus on facial looks (as blunt as that may seem).

PLUS SIZE & PETITE MODELING

Today, there are growing opportunities for plus-size people, and even petite framed people. Although the industry does not hire as many plus size or petite models as it does the more "standard" size model, especially in fashion modeling, it's still worth looking into since this is a growing market with opportunities for models to establish themselves before the field gets saturated. There are many fashion stores that sell products aimed at plus size or petite people, and they would require such models. With determination and the right attributes, you can certainly find a modeling job regardless of your build.

Chapter 3: Entering the Market

Now you know what it takes to be a professional model. You know the importance of being neat in every aspect including nails, hair, and smooth and flawless skin. You know the height requirements, and, most probably, by now you even know the kind of modeling you want to do; it could be plus size, petite, runway, nude, commercial modeling or any other, mostly depending on your attributes. Now you need to know how to enter the market.

Take Close-up Photographs for Your Portfolio

Always keep in mind that portfolio photographs are serious professional tools. Just like soldier always respects their weapons, and chefs treat their knives with the utmost care, you need to put planning and dedicated effort into these photos – since the difference between good and bad ones will determine whether you'll debut in the next Paris Fashion Week, or will be struggling to meet your rent while you take odd jobs or pose for small-time catalogs.

As with the advice meted out before, portfolio photos should be taken with minimal make-up, with foresight and planning in the arrangement of the lighting in order to highlight your best features, without any other element in the photograph, against a tasteful and/or neutral background. When you compile your portfolio, you need to ensure that you have a variety of poses and angles which would show your features and talents in the best possible manner. Try taking photographs from extreme close up to mid close up and mid ranges, so that you can adequately display your skin and structure in different lights while emitting a plethora of "attitudes" or "looks". Don't be afraid to experiment to find your look. If you're taking the picture yourself, or are asking a talented friend for help in creating your portfolio, don't hold back from taking fifty to sixty different pictures and sets — out of which you can then select the best twenty to include in the final draft which would be submitted to potential agencies and clientele.

However, preferably have a professional photographer do this for you. It may cost you a good amount of money but, if you have what it takes, the cost will be worth it. A simple search online should allow you to find local photographers who do modeling portraits. It is important to create a good portfolio from the start so that you don't have to take other photographs each time you're looking for work. Plan on carrying your portfolio with you wherever you go, and even leaving a photo or two behind whether asked to or not. If you are tech-savvy enough (or resourceful enough to do a few Google "how to" searches), I recommend having an online portfolio as well, so that you can direct potential clients straight to your website. Once you start landing decent contracts, you can always include newer photographs from each job to showcase your achievements and level of exposure in the industry, so creating new portfolios from scratch is essentially a one-time expense.

While creating your portfolios, get to work on your "walk" - which is going to be one of the very first things that agents will want to see before they sign you on. Although you'll get extensive training in this aspect once you've joined an agency, you can still check up on "walks" of established models on television and through the internet and get to work on your own. This would give you considerable advantage over other new models who are trying to get signed on, and who haven't worked on their walks either since they would be trained for it.

Know Your Measurements

At the heart of it all, the fashion industry is about matching looks with styles – it's that simple. So, if you want others to pay attention to your professionalism as a model, you need to make their job *easier* and not more difficult. In that spirit, you should know your own measurements, skin tone, body structure, etc. at the tip of your tongue so that you can answer any questions related to them at a moment's notice in case designers need to instantly determine whether you're fit for their needs or not. While the most important stats about you are your shoe size, height and weight, it does no harm to include everything else that is relevant because, that way, you will help your agent know where to place you and which clothing would fit or suit you the best. Women should know their dress sizes, for example, along with their waist, hips and bust size. Men should know their clothing measurements too, particularly waist, neck, sleeve, and chest sizes.

Remember that you always need to give the most accurate and up-to-date information regarding your physical stats, and that hyperbole and exaggeration in this industry is never tolerated and erodes your working credibility rather rapidly. Therefore, never claim to have smaller sizes than you do – since the professionals you work with would only need a moment to tell whether you're lying or not.

Approach Various Modeling Agencies

There will be several modeling agencies in your nearest city. They will often have open calls as they search for new talent. It is such opportunities for which you should be on the lookout. When going for open calls, be sure to carry your portfolio with you. The modeling agents will want you to pose or walk for them as they take a snap or two, and then you may pass or fail. The good thing is that you do not have to wait. If you did not make it, they will usually tell you right away that you did not qualify. Do not lose heart because most modeling agencies are looking for specific models, and this changes each time. You can just move on to another one. For an agent to know whether you can model or not, it takes a matter of minutes. The minute you walk into a room, they will most likely know whether you are what they are looking for.

How do you choose the best modeling agency with so many in the market and all of them claiming to be the best? You can find that out in the next chapter, which we are dedicating entirely to helping you with that. However, as a rule of thumb, always remember that while agencies could ask you for nominal fees in the beginning, the bulk of their revenue comes through commissions whenever you land a job. Therefore, irrespective of however glamorous an agency may seem from the outside, if they request you to pay them hundreds of dollars upfront for one thing or the other – you may wish to check whether or not the agency is credible or whether you're being scammed. Do not take their offers or sign any contracts before reading their small print either – regardless of any time pressure they may try to apply. Such places often succeed and get away with these endeavors primarily because they prey on the hopes and dreams of starry-eyed male and female models, who land up making bad decisions out of haste to achieve the pipe dreams spun in their heads by the scammers. Fame and fortune are undoubtedly the best blindfolds to logic and business sense.

Cultivate Your Etiquette

A professional model should have a professional demeanor. Even if you are not working in an office setting so to speak, you should still be courteous and treat people respectfully. You will be the face of many companies and products. You will have seen time and again how a small controversy can be blown out of proportion, for instance in the case of supermodels like Naomi Campbell. You will be under the spotlight quite often, and therefore circumstances demand that you demonstrate a professional attitude and appearance. Most importantly, should you make some fame and good money, don't let it get to your head.

Treat people you work with kindly. They could be making a living off you in the form of commissions, and sometimes that can get into your head. Always remember to treat them like a teammate – which is what they are – and that a recommendation from the people who know every bit of your professional life may go a long way in getting you your next gig.

You will have to be very organized. Models can be called for a photo shoot on very short notice. It is important that you don't miss any work, because there won't be work every day. Keep a day planner notebook, or use a personal assistant or scheduling phone app if need be.

You will need to establish a good working rapport with photographers. Remember, they can make or break your career, because there are often times when the clients ask the photographers who they like to work with. Be polite, ask them for tips, ask them how you can improve your pose to help make their photos better. Respect them and they will respect you. Always commend them for the good work they do. However, the sad fact is that for every ultra-professional photographer out there, there's also one exploitative one who banks on the importance of his/her connections to mistreat models. Remember that such people, more often than not, will get exposed and discredited in the industry – so don't let anyone's connections turn you into their puppet. It's better to walk away from one job and inform your client and agency about the exact nature of a problem, than to lower yourself to the standards of such people.

Once you start getting work, this is your real job, just the same as a person who has a 9 to 5 employment. If you don't take your job seriously, you will not succeed. Remember, as we said in the introduction and the first chapter, good looks are just the most basic of the requirements. Behind the glamour, there is a lot of work, a lot of learning, a lot of time invested, and a lot of maintaining a good attitude. Note that, as a model, you will most likely work for 5 years for women, and slightly more for men. Make those 5 years count.

Be Creative, and Keep Learning on the Job

Photographers will love you if you can pull off dynamic poses at different angles and with different expressions. The more variety you can offer, the better. Always show them what you have up your sleeve. Bring it, and don't be shy. When people look at your pictures, they want to see you, see some emotion, see some life, rather than just your static image.

Always think ahead, and confirm whether there would be makeup artists to help you on site. Regardless of whether you'd receive help for makeup or not, you should carry a basic makeup kit with you to every shoot. In worst case scenarios, you'll be able to apply your own makeup after understanding the kind of look needed by the photographer, and in the best case scenario you'll be able to help an on-site makeup artist with suggestions for the shades and tones which would suit you the best. If you make others' jobs easier, they will love you for it.

Chapter 4: Selecting the Right Agency

By completing the first three chapters, you are now about halfway to becoming a professional model, however we still haven't helped you select the best modeling agency for you. Before we get to that, here are a few things you need to know:

Although taking modeling classes is not a prerequisite, they may offer considerable advantages over other modeling competitors. You may have to learn a thing or two about self confidence, as you will need that when walking down the runway, watched by hundreds of people. If you feel that there is something specific you need to learn, go ahead, find a class. How much do you know about the modeling industry? Information is power. You may need to learn a few things about people skills because, while you will be the one in the spotlight, you will find that successful modeling takes a lot of teamwork. However, just as with agencies, there may exist plenty of sham classes as well. Therefore, make sure you know who's handling the teaching, as well as what exactly qualifies them to teach you in the first place. If you approach a sub-par class, it may end up doing more harm than good.

As for modeling houses, you can learn a lot about different agencies on the internet. Most modeling agencies have social media accounts where they post all their important information. Follow them on networks like Twitter and Facebook. Join internet forums where you can interact with people in the business. Even if you go to a class, you can only really glean 20% of all that you need to know. The rest you will learn on your own.

When looking for a good modeling agency, there are a few things to bear in mind. They include:

- What kind of modeling work are you looking for?

- Where you want to work as a model – as much as there is an opportunity to travel the world, are there specific cities where you would like to be grounded?

- Your ultimate modeling objectives. Do you, for example, want to become a supermodel? And so forth.

With those three factors in mind, here is how to find an agency:

Going by what type of modeling you want, start by looking for agencies that offer such kinds of modeling jobs. For example, if you want to be a commercial model, you should look for agencies that deal specifically with commercial modeling. While there may be plenty of agencies which deal with multiple modeling fields, your choice should be determined by the growth and success of each house. You may also need to consider that, while a particular multi-field agency is highly successful in their commercial modeling stream for example, they may be struggling with their fashion modeling endeavors – which is *your* preferred career stream. Therefore, you may also need to choose whether in such a case it may be better if you choose an agency that seems to be smaller than the other one in size but performs much better in the fashion modeling market. After all, an agency's job is to connect models with designers, and they can't be effective middlemen for you if they can't even approach good designers or clients in that market.

Look for an agency that has been in the business for some time. You can also look at the kind of people they work with. The more reputable a modeling agency is, the more likely it is to have the ability to get you many gigs, as we've just discussed. It's better to pay more in commission and get worthwhile gigs than to pay less and get less (or nothing).

A modeling agency gets paid when you get paid. Therefore, any agency where you are asked to put up a high upfront fee is a no-no. This is the first indication of a scam. Modeling agencies are not modeling schools and therefore they should not claim to teach you poses, diction and posture, because these can only be offered by a modeling school. The main duty of modeling agencies is to get their models and actors/actresses work. However, some of the best modeling agencies also have exclusive access to some of the best modeling schools, classes or teachers – since they would logically want their own models to be better trained than their business competitors. Therefore, when you're attempting to choose between modeling houses, also inquire about availability or access to good modeling classes which they can provide for you. Regardless, you still wouldn't need to pay the agency the fees, and so any request by them for you to pay the same upfront should be a red flag for you.

What are your goals in modeling? Let's assume for an example that you are looking for an opportunity to model in some countries in Eastern Europe. You should thus look for agencies that can get you work there. If you live in New York and you would only like to work there, then you should look for local agencies. It is important that you let your agent know your objectives early on.

Look for modeling agencies' reviews on the internet. That way you can find out what other people think about the agency. You won't be entering deals with them blindly. If you find even one reasonable negative review about an agency, use your judgment and decide if it's enough to make you avoid that agency. You can always move on to another agency.

Lastly, will you work with a small or a big agency? If you are just starting out, it may be beneficial to work with a smaller agency. You will have less competition and you can have more attention from your agent. You may also be given some great opportunities to be mentored elsewhere on posture, diction, gait and so on, as your agent will want to get the best out of you. This is unlike the bigger agencies, which will just let you go if you make a few mistakes.

How much should you pay your agency? Genuine agencies are paid on a commission basis, they get paid when you get paid. The fee varies, but the rate is typically 15 to 20%. If a modeling agency charges much less than the standard market rate, please be wary – you could be in for a scam. In addition to the agreed commission, you may have to face more cuts from your first pay, especially if the agency invested in upfront costs on your behalf, for example if they helped prepare your portfolio or paid a photographer for a test shoot.

One important point – any legitimate business will have no problem giving you time to read through their contract. If you've been handed one, and feel pressured by them to sign right away, you should be especially careful about this point. Many models have found themselves in the talons of exploitative or sham businesses simply because they didn't have the foresight to read the small print. So, once you've had your meeting with an agency, go back home with the contract before you sign, and go through it with someone who may have a better understanding of such matters than you.

Chapter 5: Staying Successful

From the prior chapters, you now know how to get started in modeling. And now in this chapter, we will help turn you into a professional. The most important thing is to get started though, and the rest is a learning experience. Once you get your first gig, you will see that there is always room for growth. Continuous practice and training will eventually turn you into a professional.

Being a professional model is very hard work. It is difficult to enter the profession and it is even harder to stay there. Sometimes there is work and sometimes there isn't. Sometimes, the schedules are so hectic and grueling such that you don't even have time to pack properly, moving from one shoot to another. It is therefore important that you know a few things that all professional models know.

1. Professional models know how to pack fast, at a moment's notice. They know how to travel light and, most importantly, they know how to stay in job mode all the time, as if they are waiting for a call to come.

2. Professional models keep on learning all the time. Just because you are a professional does not mean that you know everything. Like any other career, modeling is very dynamic, changing all the time. Keep on top of things, learn all you can, and make friendships with people who are in the same career.

3. Never let your ego or pride dictate your relationship with others. Your good looks won't last long enough to make that worth it. Cultivate your brains instead.

4. Location, location and more location is very important for a model, perhaps just as important as it is for a real estate developer. What this means is that if you live in a small, secluded country town, chances are that you will never be discovered, even if you meet the gorgeous, slim, tall and graceful qualifications of a professional model. However, cities like London, New York, Milan and Paris, to name but a few, will place you in a better position to be noticed.

5. Once you enter the professional modeling field, treat it as your full time, serious job. Find ways to get better, never be late for appointments and, most important, try to be a positive, energetic, and enthusiastic person, with a friendly and respectful attitude. If you burn out after a late night out, you will not make it far in this field. Sometimes you may have to repeat the same pose for hours on end, until the director feels that they have what they need. All those glamorous pictures that you see on magazine covers are products of rigorous, uncomfortable, backbreaking work.

6. Always try to make work easier for the directors and photographers. These are the people who shape opinions about a model, and can get you more work – or prevent you from getting more work. Therefore, if you can keep them happy by making their jobs easier, they will help you to pave your way to high status assignments.

7. You are in modeling to make money and therefore not every deal is good enough for you. Remember, you will most likely

only be at the prime of your career for five years before your modeling star will start fading. For a client to part with those precious dollars to promote his company, product or service, you must be willing to give them the best. Be the best you can be, give your all, and, as far as it rests with you, make sure that when you get out of the industry, you will be missed.

8. That you have a good agent does not mean that there will always be work. The buck stops right with you. When you meet clients, show courtesy, let them see the model when you walk in. Spit out that chewing gum, be neat, dress nicely and be willing to change where necessary.

9. You will face a lot of criticism in your career. Do you have the strength to stand through it all? Some of it can be malicious and some can be very constructive. It is up to you to take what is useful and discard the rest. Professional models are driven by self esteem, confidence and skill. Don't let anyone ruin that for you.

10. Keep aside some money, as much as you can save. Professional modeling can be a short-lived career, with some seasons being very low. In addition, you will only be at your career prime for five years and then you will be out of the business. Save up for the times when you don't have the work.

11. Professional modeling is a people-skills business. You should be prepared to meet a lot of people. If your objective is to become a commercial model, you may have to learn some acting skills so that you can pull off television commercials perfectly.

12. Learn to concentrate on the job. Your job is important. It is best to give it all the attention it deserves. If you are good at your first job, it will get you that second job, that may get you your third job, and so on. Just remember that you have to get better after every job.

13. Always keep an open mind. It is not wise to focus solely on fashion, editorial and runway modeling. Those fields are very

competitive, and it may be a long time before you get yourself a job. There is more to modeling. For example, commercial modeling offers far more opportunities than fashion modeling does.

14. You should prepare for an exit strategy out of modeling. It will not last forever. Therefore, if directors keep telling you how good you are at acting for television commercials, maybe you should consider a transition into an acting career later in life. You can be many things rolled into one package.

15. Look at fashion magazines. These are resources which can give you great tips for modeling. You can learn poses and body postures. While you're at it, practice some poses in front of your mirror.

Conclusion

Well, I hope this book will help turn you from a wannabe model to a professional, and that your life will never be the same again. Professional modeling is one of the few well paid careers for which you do not need to have a college degree. This does not mean that if you are spotted when in school you should simply drop out and bring your education to a half. You can either model while still in school, or postpone school for a few years, especially since you probably only have five prime years in modeling, and then they will look for fresh talent.

If entering the modeling industry is hard, staying there is even harder, but don't worry. Even the big names like Tyra Banks and Naomi Campbell started somewhere. If you are turned down, don't be disappointed and never forget to be courteous. You never know, it could be that next week they're searching for someone exactly like you. Courtesy truly is your calling card. You need to be a sport to work with, so make the directors and the photographers love you. As much as you are more beautiful than most people, you need not be a grouch or a prima donna. Be a people person, because modeling is a people career. Above all, avoid falling into a comfort zone, and learn more ways to make your modeling pay. Be creative and try as many poses and body postures as you can. When your knowledge provides for greater flexibility and ease trying different things, you make it easy for your director and photographers, and they love you the more for it.

Once your modeling career prime starts fading, you may want to consider moving on from this industry while you're still at your peak, rather than pushed out when you're past your prime. This would allow you to leave on your own terms, and give you far more influence than if you were edged out. Ex-models, owing to their high level of exposure, often find great careers in television and movies if not in fashion editorials, magazines, etc. If you had the next step of your life already planned out, you may be considering finishing your schooling – which is an awesome idea if you wish to enter a specific job stream – but if you don't, then you may want to join acting classes or polish up other professional skills while you have time so that you can proceed to other, greener pastures. Many successful ex-models even go on to form their own agencies, which is an option that will require considerable networking from you while you're still working. Remember that there will always be a way for you to stay relevant in the field, as long as you apply yourself to your plan with complete dedication.

Last, I'd like to thank you for purchasing this book! If you enjoyed it or found it helpful, I'd greatly appreciate it if you'd take a moment to leave a review on Amazon. Thank you!